Daisy Chains

Harvey Sagar

Published by Harvey Sagar 2015

ISBN 978-0-9575537-9-8

Other works by the author include:

1. *Teddy Bear's Triumph: Tales from a Medical Allotment*

2. *DRY Out!*

3. *Come Rhyme With Me*

4. *Lines to the Lost*

www.harveysagararts.com

To Daisy

Contents

Page

The Race

One day at school, we had a running race;
I started off quite well but then fell flat upon my face.
The reason was quite clear: that clumsy Billy Fleet
Had juxtaposed his trainer in the midst of my two feet.

I felt the greatest pain that anyone could experience
Though without cuts or bruising or change in my
appearance.
The teacher said she felt that much more my pride was
sore
But I didn't know where to find it so couldn't comment
more.

Needless to say, I lost the race and Billy came in first.
I didn't feel resentment though I wished his gut would
burst.
Teacher said that I should try to take it philosophically;
I don't know if I did but I planned Billy's murder
periodically.

Someone told me not to worry and the next race I would
win
Provided I made sure to keep the ground far from my
chin.
My idea of what to do to give me the greatest chance
Was to sew a nuclear bomb into Billy's underpants.

I was very good; I brooded only for eight weeks;
My height of anger varied though had smaller troughs
than peaks.
Then something happened that would all my gloom
allay:
We started doing casting for our annual Christmas play.

The teacher eyed us up to decide which parts would best
Complement our natures and our talents truly test.
I was cast as Cinderella, of all the roles the best;
Billy was in the chorus along with all the rest.

The Swimming Lesson

When we got in the pool, I felt I was freezing;
My friend next to me was shivering and sneezing.
The swimming instructor said we'd soon all be warm,
Once into lesson and new strokes we'd performed.

She told us that learning to swim would be great
And soon we would find all our fears would abate.
We'd have lots of fun, once we'd learned to stop crying;
And, at the seaside, the skill might just keep us from
dying.

I'd heard it before but still did not feel that bold
And my friend, still sneezing, said she'd just caught a
cold.
I was fond of her but felt I had to break free
Because I did not want her to give it to me.

By luck, I was moved to a group near the door
Of brave children who'd had one or two lessons before.
My friend, with her germs, was left with the others:
First lesson, all frightened, indulged by their mothers.

All courage regained, I set off down the pool.
At least what we did was a break from the school.
After a while, I sensed we'd achieved a big feat
But, when I looked up, we'd only travelled six feet.

Still, our instructor said we'd achieved a great deal;
As a reward, she'd teach us to do water cartwheels:
Force our heads in the water to an imaginary hollow
And move the body in a circle so our legs would just
follow.

I banged my face on the tiles at the bottom
And immediately sensed I'd encountered a problem.
The pain in my mouth displayed a hard truth
That I had just broken an incisor tooth.

I came to the surface, in agony and bleeding;
A great deal of cosseting I felt I was needing.
I told the teacher acute treatment was pressing
But she just asked if I wanted to continue the lesson.

From that moment on, I felt quite discouraged
And anyway the exercise made me feel undernourished.
I decided to give up the swimming for good
And, once my mouth's fully healed, just to focus on food.

First Day at School

I remember the first day that I went to school;
Mum kissed me and said she'd see me again soon.
She said that I would find lots of friends
But I saw none despite searching from morning 'til noon.

The teacher seemed nice but she looked like my grandma
Except that I never saw a smile leave her face.
Like my grandma, her voice was high-pitched and posh
But her clothes were different: just drab, a disgrace.

I sat next to a girl who did little but scratch
And things like earwigs ran free through her hair.
I remember seeing little insects like that
At the zoo, when Mum made me look at a bear.

Later on in the morning, we had to do painting;
Teacher said we should create from our heart.
That scared me because I thought she meant blood,
So my creation was doomed from the start.

The boy on my right said his name was Bon Jovi
And to be honest I found it hard to believe him.
When he said his Dad was Mayor of New York,
I knew that he was just daft, stupid and dim.

At least we had lunch though I can't say it was great;
The meat was like cardboard and the chips were all wet.
Like the fool that he was, Bon Jovi swallowed it all.
He'd eat the knives and the forks, if he could, I would bet.

As we travelled back home, Mum asked how it had been
And if my day had been filled with new things and fun.
She asked what had been the best thing of the day;
I thought hard before choosing the tea and cream bun.

Trip to the Country

Grandma told me that, when she was a child,
There was a pond at the end of the road.
She said that there she'd see sticklebacks,
Rosebay willow herb, newts, frogs and toads.

But now it's a land made of concrete,
With a supermarket at either end.
The wildlife has fled to the country;
The car has become our new friend.

But in a park she showed me some sparrows;
Not only that but a chaffinch as well.
She told me that, if I used my eyes and my ears,
I'd find more than even Grandad could tell.

So I looked round about and saw a red bird;
I heard another bird sing in the sky.
I knew the white birds on the river were swans
But I'd never before seen them fly.

We ate sandwiches on the banks of the water
And saw a small bird with its nose in the stream.
When I looked up, something bright blue flashed by;
The river glistened and I started to dream.

I saw big green fields and a forest of trees;
I saw me asleep with a fox;
I saw brown cows eating in herds;
And sheep cuddled together in flocks.

I travelled back home in the back of the car
To my home where there's no grass in sight.
But I determined I'd for ever go back
To the place filled with joy, sound and light.

Camping in Scotland

Every summer, when I was a kid,
We'd fill up the car with mad stuff;
A boot so full it could barely be closed
And a roof rack, as if the rest weren't enough.

As children, as usual, we sat in the back,
Piled high with duvets and blankets.
At our feet was carried enough food for an army,
Apparently for great outdoor banquets.

We'd pack waterproofs, T-shirts, trainers and boots
To cater for all kinds of weather.
We learned that our climax of holiday bliss
Would be treks across Scottish heather.

Some days there was rain, others snow, hail or wind,
Though I admit we sometimes saw sun.
On the walks, they fed us with Kendall mint cake,
Which they said boosts energy and fun.

The tent was about as big as my bedroom
But had to sleep four, not just me.
If I needed the go to the loo in the nighttime,
I had to crawl out of the tent for a pee.

Some days we climbed mountains and got to a place
So high, down the cliff you could plummet.
But then they would say there's more walking to do;
That spot was just a false summit.

One year, we went to Scotland in August
Instead of our usual June.
I was bitten to death by monster-sized midges
And lived the week in a constant monsoon.

When I am older and have kids of my own,
I'll remember those days, wild and free.
I'll go back to the hills but find a five-star hotel,
With views of the sand and the sea.

Nativity Play

When I was six, we planned a nativity play
In which the whole school would take part.
All our parents and friends were invited
To see a creation of music and art.

At least, that's what the teachers all told us;
They said that we'd all be so proud.
We had to remember to stick to our roles,
Not to fidget or sing out too loud.

Mrs. Dixon was in charge of the casting
And she wrote down the words that we'd say.
But our parents had to make all our costumes;
Dad asked if it was he who must pay.

Mrs. D thought that I could be Mary
And Joseph should be Kathy McShane.
I said that Kath was a girl, but Joseph a man,
But she said it was all much the same.

Mum made me a dress of old bedsheets
With a shawl of discarded bath towel.
The family bible she placed in my hands
And said I should smile and not scowl.

When the big day came, I stood on the stage,
With a doll on some straw, baby Jesus.
I trembled and cried and forgot all my lines
But Mum said my performance was genius.

As a treat, we then went to McDonald's
And I thought back to the things we'd been taught.
I prayed this was not my last supper
And that Mum a lot more food had bought.

We Made Cakes

Our teacher said we would do something called cook
And said don't shy away; it was well worth a look.
I was surprised, as I think were most of the others,
Because we thought that was done only by mothers.

When I told that to Dad, he did nothing but laugh
And said that I'd made something, I think called a gaff.
When he explained, I said, no, we'd made no mistakes
And anyway the teacher said we were going to bake
cakes.

He said that those views were not allowed to exist
Because, when an adult, they were something called
sexist.
I could not see how cakes could create such a fuss
But he said it was about mothers that the things were
unjust.

Anyway, next day back at school we did baking
And all kinds of funny food were there for the taking.
We threw flour, eggs and sugar in a massive great bowl
And stirred it all round with a big wooden pole.

Then we put lumps of the stuff on a flat metal tray
And it looked really horrid, of that I must say.
Teacher said it'd be great when it comes out the oven;
Then we could decorate it with nice chocolate buttons.

When we had finished, we could take some of them
home,
Having added to each lots of a rich, creamy foam.
Apart from the chocolate, we added sparkles and fruit.
Teacher said our cooking skills no-one could dispute.

I gave one to Dad and he took a big bite;
He smiled and his face just seemed to alight.
He couldn't resist to gorge down another;
Then said that my cooking was as good as my mother's.

I Lost My Teddy Bear

Once, in a playground, I lost my teddy bear;
I thought he had left me for ever.
I cried like a fountain, snuggled up in my bed
And I thought I might hide there for ever.

Then my best friend, the owl, fell onto the pillow;
He was cuddly, soft, warm and kind.
He usually sat on the top of the headboard
But he came down to sort out my mind.

Some say that toy animals are not able to speak
But I knew he was talking to me.
He told me Teddy would return as before;
He'll be back again, just wait and see.

I went off to sleep, dreamt of eating ice cream,
Which with joy I shared with my bear.
Then Teddy said, "Snooze; I'll see you again in the morning"
But, on wakening, he was not there.

I searched round the playground to see where he was
But found only crisp packets and cans.
In sadness, I went home and walked round the garden,
Wishing Teddy was there in my hands.

And there by the garage I found him asleep;
I gave him my dearest embraces.
Sometimes one who is lost can give us surprise
By coming back in the strangest of places.

I Know You're a Child

I know you're a child but soon you will grow;
You'll discover the world and its treasures.
There's so much to explore, so much to learn;
New future, new friendships, new pleasures.

In a few years, I know that you will look back
At the first time you saw the sun rise;
At the first time you read a book all way through;
At the first time you had burger and fries.

But meanwhile you'll have many great birthday parties,
With friends in fancy dresses quite mad,
Where you all sing and dance and your parent hangs
round,
Looking useless and frankly quite sad.

Everyone will tell you you must do well at school
And to be honest it's not bad advice.
But I know that you will seek other ventures;
That's good but sometimes think twice.

You may feel it's all sorted but there are years still to
come
So save up some thoughts to make your life smoother.
Don't sacrifice now what you may need to hold dear
To help you build life to an enriching future.

My Pet

One of our neighbours had a big furry cat;
I liked it; in fact, I was smitten.
One day, her owner told me with glee
That the cat had just had four kittens.

Each of the four looked just like their Mum
But obviously quite a bit smaller.
I picked one of them up and give it a kiss
And asked what her Mummy would call her.

The lady told me that no name had been chosen
But I could pick any one that I liked.
I cuddled the kitten and looked into her eyes
And said, "What do you think about Mike?"

Our neighbour was kindly; she'd a big rosey face
And a stomach like on overgrown snowman.
She chuckled, bent down, looked into my eyes
And said, "If you want to call her that, then you can."

I think I held onto that kitten for five or six hours
Though the lady thought it ten minutes.
Sometimes she told me not to squeeze it so tight
Especially when the cat grimaced.

I think she sensed that we were inseparable
Because she said she might give me a present;
If my parents approved, I could take Mike back home
Provided I gave the kitten love and not torment.

I ran all the way home and bumped into my Dad
And excitedly told what I'd heard;
But he said no cat was to live in his house;
Instead he would buy me a bird.

So we chose a blue budgie, who spent all day in a cage;
It was a bit hard to see what to like.
But I often went round to see the kittens grow up
And at least I called the bird Mike.

Cycling

One Christmas, my parents bought me a bike
And said now I should learn to cycle.
In the country, I would find lots of things I would like;
Much better than sitting home idle.

I was pleased because Sophie already had one
And had treated me as someone inferior.
Now I knew I'd be matched at least as an equal
Though, in my mind, quite possibly superior.

Mum said that soon we could go out as a couple
And have fun when she'd finished work.
Dad said he'd give me all of the lessons
I needed to not go beserk.

On my first lesson out, I was stumbling and swerving,
When Sophie rode past with loud cheers.
I comforted myself with one simple thought:
That my cycle was newer than hers.

I would ride my bike, with Dad holding on at the back,
Making sure I did not fall over.
The first time he let go, to see if I could balance,
I tumbled and got a mouth full of clover.

As luck would have it, Sophie was there on her bike
And could hardly contain raucous laughter.
I determined that I'd be a better cycler than her,
If not tomorrow, then at least some time after.

It happened that, at last, I could finally balance
And could ride without Dad's support.
Mum and I used to go out in the evenings;
At speed round the parks we'd cavort.

Some years later, I was in competition
At a cycling race for the County.
Sophie was also a competitor there;
She came second but I won the bounty.

Learning Languages

When we went up to our new school, we began to learn French
And to stop speaking English was a bit of a wrench.
We also did Spanish and some German too;
They told us linguistic skills we'd accrue.

French had lots of new rules, including something called grammar
Though when teacher first said it, I thought she talked about Grandma.
There were lots of strange words that no-one could pronounce.
Each week, it seemed, some new rule she'd announce.

They said we should practise, as part of our homework,
So, with friends, I went to our local McDonald's.
I asked for a burger with "pommes de terre frites";
The guy responded by asking if I'd like cheese or just meat.

When my food arrived, I said thank you with "Merci"
But I think that he mistook my statement as "Mercy!"
With horror, he asked what was wrong with my meal
And was it just sandwich or the bargain meal deal?

Spanish is weird, I get my lip movements jumbled
So most of my speech seems to come out all mumbled.
All the words seem to end in "os", "as" or "o"
Like "buenos dias"and "mucho gusto".

Speaking German is worse; it feels like I'm barking
And there's one more thing that I think worth's
remarking:
Most people back home of the language seem clueless
And, with no German holidays, the learning is useless.

My friend said her Dad had told her don't worry;
There's no need to learn foreign, at least in a hurry;
But I feel reluctant to agree when he says not to care
Because English is spoken just about everywhere.

My First Boyfriend

I was just turned twelve, not long at new school,
When I started to receive attention from boys.
Perhaps a mistake, but I told all to my Dad;
His reaction implied I should stick to my toys.

One guy called Jake would not leave me alone;
He was always there, attentive and fawning.
He asked me to share in a trip to the park;
I told Dad but, while frowning, he gave me a warning.

He told me that, yes, I should spend time with boys
And such relationships were all perfectly natural.
But there was a time and a place for all things in life;
Right now, it was schoolwork; he was just being factual.

A few weeks later, we had a school outing
To some animal park, a few miles from town.
I sat next to Jake on the bus there and back;
He was fun though admittedly a bit of a clown.

Everyone on the bus was talking and laughing;
We made lots of jokes and sang lots of songs.
Jake's voice was great; he was like a rock star;
It seemed he could never do anything wrong.

But next day at school, he was with someone else
Whom I'd considered a close friend, called Julie.
He was sidled up close, smiling and whispering;
I was saddened, distraught, really, truly.

I hurried back home at the end of the day
And in tears collapsed into Dad's open arms.
I felt better when he said there were more fish in the sea
And always be cautious with a man's blatant charms.

My First Girlfriend

If I'd known then all the things I know now,
I don't think I would have gone near her.
But I spied her one day staring into her phone
And at once knew no love could be dearer.

Just outside school, I saw she was waiting
For her friend to walk together back home.
I approached her and asked if, instead of her friend,
With me through the park she might like to roam.

She was cute with that mop of shining black hair
And I felt sure that her eyes searched my mind.
She had a great laugh and teeth better than mine;
Definitely sexy but maybe also quite kind.

I knew she was the one and her love I must win
So we never would part and be together forever.
To the greatest of joys, she agreed to come with me
So all I need do was pursue with endeavour.

We walked round the park and I knew me she fancied.
I entertained her with jokes, silly stories and jesting.
I sensed that she thought me the one that she'd want,
Even though she spent most of the time texting.

She didn't say much even though I kept talking
And I stuck to subjects nice, clean and healthy.
She did speak just once, when we stopped by the bandstand,
To tell me she wanted to photo a selfie.

She then used her phone to send off the picture
And I suddenly felt anxious, I will not pretend.
She spoke just once more when I asked whom she'd texted
And she told me she'd sent it to her boyfriend.

I knew it was over, all my hopes had been dashed;
Any progress with her would be just a grind.
But I consoled myself with one comforting thought:
That at least it was not me who'd been badly two-timed.

Grandma

Grandma once told me she'd had just one boyfriend;
That is, till she'd acquired her second.
She went on to have just one or two more;
In the end, a few more than she'd reckoned.

She stressed that in choosing she'd always been careful
And that I must do just the same.
Character and virtue were things that she valued;
Avoid people who treat love as a game.

Don't dive in headlong and take care where you land
And she wasn't referring to swimming.
Be especially careful if, for someone you meet,
At once your love seems just brimming.

She said that even the best friends break up,
Whoever they are, boys or girls.
And that can create sadness, frankly even despair
But out there, you can find a new world.

She said I was young and she might be speaking too soon
But to be forewarned is forearmed.
Apparently life would bring great experience
And she wanted to shield me from harm.

She said I might end up having quite a few boyfriends
Before meeting someone I'd stay with for years.
She hoped that the right person I would stay with for
ever,
Though relationships can end in tears.

But I must enjoy what I've had and respect all the people
I've met
And benefit from those who've been close.
And when I meet the right person, she hoped that I'd
find
More joy than I could ever suppose.

Bullies and Friends

Someone at school was really nasty to me,
Though I'd no idea who he was.
He picked on me in the playground at lunch
And pinched me for no reason, no cause.

On another day, teacher told us to draw
Something that reminded us of fun days.
I made an image of me on the sand,
With my Dad asleep, in a daze.

But the boy on my left gazed down at my picture
And then laughed and said I was useless.
He told me his drawing of their dog was just brilliant,
While I lacked imagination, just clueless.

On so many days, other kids gave me pain;
They just picked on me like a servant.
I hoped that the teachers would give me support
But they were helpless or just unobservant.

I remember one day when I stood by the gates
With an ice cream I'd bought from a van.
This horrible boy pushed it all in my face
And once again my sorrow began.

I was still crying when Dad picked me up in the car
And even later with a McDonald's burger.
I hated those boys who'd been nasty to me
And thought revenge, hard torture and murder.

But back at home, I got out of the car
And Annie, my neighbour was waiting.
Though aged only four, she gave a big cuddle
And at once my fears were abating.

Asleep

Sometimes when I'm falling off to sleep,
It's dark and I see monsters.
I cry out loud; Dad puts on the lights
And tells me I'm just bonkers.

One night I dreamt that I was drowning,
In a river, nearly dead.
I cried out loud; Dad put on the lights
And said I'd wet the bed.

On another night, I lay in snow;
I was dying, and nearly froze.
I cried out loud; Dad put on the lights,
Put back discarded bedclothes.

One time, a lion jumped onto my bed;
It was ferocious, hairy and fat.
I cried out loud; Dad put on the lights
And kicked out our overfed cat.

I don't know why I'm attacked in the night
But at least I know what to do:
I cry out loud; Dad puts on the lights
And tells me to just sleep it through.

He says that I must close my eyes
And make my mind go blank.
Truthfully though that's oh so boring;
Monsters are better, to be frank.

My Brother

I was older than my brother,
By four years, I think, at least.
As a young girl, I was lovely,
While he was quite a beast.

I behaved just so perfectly
And was demure with pose,
While he pulled legs off spiders
Or sat and picked his nose.

My clothes were all designer
From the top range of Primark;
His were frankly awful,
Just football shirts, all stark.

At eight, I did fine art
And studied archeology,
While he ran round like mad,
The family's great apology.

As a teen, I sought a future;
He lived on roller skates
And wasted time with friends,
While I had lots of dates.

I aspired to be a lawyer
And married at twenty-two,
While he just went off travelling -
Could never see it through.

Now I'm still so happy,
While he is just quite sad.
My Tesco job's a bonus;
His priesthood's just a fad.

I like my council flat
And do not miss my spouse;
My brother's wife can't cope
In their neo-Georgian house.

Now, my brother when he speaks
About the past, it is quite strange,
Not least because he says
My memory's deranged.

Teenagers

Teenagers can be troublesome;
Even you must know that's true.
It's all to do with hormones
And finding out what's you.

You can sometimes feel aggression;
You may feel that life's not fair;
You may feel they're all against you;
But you've love that you can share.

The road may seem uneven
And you'll trip along the way;
But if you just keep going,
You'll find you'll have your say.

Just share your life with others,
The troubles and the joys.
Keep close the things that matter
And shutter out the noise.

Right now, the world seems hard
But you're an adult in the making.
You may struggle through the ups and downs
But, in the end, the life's worth taking.

You may think that now will always be
But there will also be tomorrow.
A life of huge potential's there;
You need not feel just sorrow.

My Child Asleep

I gazed onto the bed and saw my child asleep;
She looked so calm and peaceful, no problems with the
world.
I wondered what might be coursing through her dreams,
What new adventure, new anxiety, might soon become
unfurled.

Tomorrow would be normal, more kisses, laughs and
hugs;
More walking, stumbling, laughing, playing, lots of food
and drink.
From that one small body, my mind was filled with
visions
And anxieties that one day these high spots all would
sink.

In this year, there'd be a birthday, lots of presents, lots of
laughter;
My little girl in a silly hat and a dress of pink, frilled
satin;

She and her friends at a party and play on a bouncy
castle;
I just pray that these wonderful peaks of joy will never
ever flatten.

In the summer, we'll go on holiday to a beach and eat ice
cream.
She'll strut across the beach and through the surf,
demeanour of a queen.
Then she'll fall asleep in the sun; we'll move the shade to
cover her.
Long may these moments last, the greatest treasures I've
ever seen.

Each year she'll grow, she'll go to school, new people she
will meet;
She'll learn new things about the world, some good but
sometimes bad.
I fear my bond with her with time will slowly weaken
And all that will be left for me are memories of what
we've had.

But who can guess the future, what the next day's going to bring?
You might as well anticipate joy, as much as you do dread.
In the meantime, what's for sure is that you're blessed with something great:
A beautiful child, all curled up, and dreaming in her bed.

My City Centre

Sometimes with friends I'd hang around town,
Though Dad said it might not be the best.
He'd stare into my eyes and say with a frown
That we might find we were put to the test.

I don't know what he meant but he said there were
dangers
So just stay in places near people;
Make sure to shun all advances from strangers;
Look confident, not appealing or feeble.

Once we were standing in the road next to Primark.
I looked round to see what he meant.
It was about nine o'clock and getting quite dark
But I felt no great danger or torment.

Admittedly, down the road was a bar,

Where all kinds of street life were gathering.

They were shouting and screaming, doing things quite

bizarre;

Many were vomiting and staggering.

We moved up a side street to a park near a church,

Where girls stood by the side of the road.

A driver moved slowly and stopped at the verge;

Promise of money to a girl he bestowed.

On the pavement just opposite, a girl was engaged

In a deal; he gave her a packet

Of white powder; she looked quite deranged;

He stuffed her money deep in his jacket.

We thought we'd best leave and maybe go for a drink

But none of us had any cash;

No bus fare either, so we walked through the park

But then we saw a creepy guy flash.

When we got nearer home, I said goodnight to my
friends
And pondered on the night we'd just spent.
To be honest, I felt glad it had come to an end
And understood just what my Dad meant.

A Trial at Age Twelve

When I was about twelve, I felt suddenly frightened;
It seemed overnight all my emotions were heightened.
Some of the time, like before, I felt glad
But a lot of the time I was downbeat and sad.

Some kids in my class said I was no longer much fun,
So I felt so much better when the school day was done.
But I often went home and stayed in my room
And played with my Ipad to break free of the gloom.

Some guy posted my Facebook and asked to be friend;
He'd been lonely for ages and looked for an end
To a long life of boredom, for some pleasure to see,
And he hoped that he find it in conversation with me.

We exchanged a few messages and then lots of texts
But gradually the subjects changed to ones about sex.
For a while, seeking friendship, I felt inclined to respond
But suddenly, one day, some awareness just dawned.

I remembered one class that we'd had at our school,
Which taught us the internet can treat us like fools.
They told us that strangers can try to get close,
Not simply for friendship but for something more gross.

I told my Mum and my Dad and they told the police;
They said they knew of this guy and his ventures would
cease.
Once they'd proven their case, he'd be locked away;
Meanwhile I with childhood adventures should stay.

I have to say I didn't feel better straight away
But my mood did lighten with each passing day.
My parents said that I must always look forward,
When gradually life would appear much less awkward.

Musical Experiences

I don't know whether it was my idea or theirs
But someone thought I should be more creative;
Do something that would bring me out of myself
And make me more assertive, less plaintive.

They thought a good thing was absorption with music,
So I should apply myself to an instrument.
I was keen when they suggested that I learn the piano
But was less sure when the lessons were imminent.

Mrs. Gyde was the teacher and was nice but quite strict.
She showed me the black and white keys;
She talked about naturals, keys, sharps and flats
But it all went over my head like a breeze.

I couldn't believe that my right hand played one thing,
While my left hand did something quite diffcrent;
Not only that but my feet also played pedals.
I gave effort but it seems insufficient.

I asked Mum and Dad if I could try something easier
So they suggested I play the guitar.
But I found once again the two hands did things
different;
The similarity was really bizarre.

A couple of years later, I turned to the flute,
Which with each step gave only one note.
The trouble was you had to get your lips right
Or no sound at all you'd promote.

So I turned to the drums and could cope with the
rhythms
And had no melody to worry about;
But the neighbours were less keen than me with the noise
And demanded that my kit I throw out.

So in the end I turned to an Ipod with earphones;
I chose the music and felt quite creative.
No-one else needed to share in my ventures
And I could cut out those behaviours abrasive.

My Bedroom

When Mum or Dad was horrible to me,
I would like to go to my bedroom.
There I had all my friends gathered round,
Who'd work to dispel all my gloom.

There was Dolly, Hank Hedgehog and Bobby the Bear,
Two stuffed penguins and a pink rocking horse.
They'd cuddle up close, show me comfort and rest
And give advice as a matter of course.

When a bit older, these friends were still there
And they shared with my Ipad and phone.
They liked to take selfies with me in the frame.
They stayed with me until I had grown.

Sometimes, as a teen, school mates were quite nasty;
I'd feel hurt and cry all the way home.
Mum and Dad showed me love; each gave kisses and
hugs
But it was in my bedroom I felt never alone.

Since then I've had boyfriends, some better than others;
Some a bit casual and others quite keen.
But one thing I know, at least up to now:
In my bedroom are the best friends I've seen.

I told Dad and he said it wouldn't be always like that,
That I'd mature and mix with the crowds.
But as long as my bedroom gives a sanctuary to me,
I'll just live with my head in the clouds.

The IQ Test

They warned us that the whole school would be doing a
test,
Designed to find out just how clever we were,
Not as individuals but for the group as a whole;
We must each do our best and with no-one confer.

They said we'd be doing research for the country,
That our efforts would lead to improvements in teaching.
Lots of other schools would do the same test;
The results would be novel, profound and outreaching.

Mrs. Biggs said ours would take place on Tuesday;
We'd spend one or two hours with no food or drink;
We were not allowed to go out of the room;
If stuck on a question, we should just sit and think.

I asked what to do if I needed the loo;
She said to keep still, body upright, cross-legged.
But, if I thought I might soon wet myself,
Someone would go with me, provided I begged.

Me and my friends thought that it sounded just stupid
And had no inclination to join in at all.
But we knew, in the end, we had really no choice,
So we worked out how we could make it all stall.

They told us there were about eighty questions,
Spread across several pages and all numbered in order.
We were basically good children but could not resist
Creation of an outcome of maximal disorder.

In the end, we decided, whatever the question,
We would all give exactly the same answer.
To questions six, seven, eight, nine and ten,
Our responses would be "Top class ballet dancers".

For questions that numbered thirteen, fourteen, eighteen,
We'd give a reply "Pacific island, New Guinea".
For all those from sixty-five to the end,
It'd be "My Mum's latest floral silk pinny".

Sad for us all, the teachers heard in advance

Of the elaborate plans we'd so carefully constructed.

We abandoned them all when they threatened dire
outcome,

If we persisted with our plans and such behaviour
conducted.

Christmas

We put up the tree about two weeks before Christmas
And, in decoration, I did most of the work.
I think I put on about three or four baubles,
While Grandma did nothing but talk.

Admittedly, Dad put the tree in the pot
And made it secure in some soil.
Mum did the rest of the baubles, the ribbons and lights
And, yes, thanked me for all my hard toil.

Some decorations were like little caves,
With interiors shining and bright.
Each day I loved to stare at the insides,
Where I saw fairies, coloured and bright.

At the edge of the branches were foils full of chocolate,
Which Dad said we could have "by and by".
I thought it mean just to give me temptation
When I only wanted to eat four or five.

Father Christmas at the scout hut was jolly and kind
Though he said. "Ho, ho, ho" quite a lot.
He wanted to know what to bring me for Christmas
So I asked for Simon Cowell's yacht.

Dad said I was cheeky and should say something proper
So I asked for a small baby brother.
For some reason, Dad looked shocked to the core
And said I should think of another.

Back at the tree, I told the fairies my plight
That, in a panic, I'd asked for a teddy.
I told them that I already had three or four
And for another was not really ready.

They told me that I should calm all my woes,
That they would put it all right.
On Christmas Eve, my worries kept me awake;
I don't think that I slept the whole night.

But nonetheless, it seemed Father Christmas did come
Because my stocking was filled with wrapped presents.
I opened them all but kept the biggest till last:
A teddy bear smelling of scent.

At first, I was crying but Teddy cuddled up close
And my new friend I started to like.
But I still felt a bit sad as I went down the stairs
'Til Dad showed me my shining new bike.

New Year's Eve

When I was thirteen, I spent New Year with Grandma;
She said that she'd let me stay up quite late.
Each year before, I was in bed by midnight,
So for the New Year I had until next day to wait.

Sometimes, the morning did not seem that great
Because, as usual, I would wake about seven.
All the rest of the family were still fast asleep
And gave no sign of life at least till eleven.

When I was younger, I'd just sit in my bed;
While waiting for family, I would talk with my toys.
I admit that last year, still early to bed,
In the morning, I was thinking much more about boys.

Grandma said that we would start with a meal,
With food that she thought I'd find scrumptious.
After that, we'd play games, then dance for a while
But I must stay awake and not get tetchy or bumptious.

For some reason, that I still don't quite understand,
The food, the music and dance were all Scottish.
I wondered if the English did not perceive the New Year
But sensed that Grandma partied with polish.

I'd have been happy for the TV to be turned on at six;
However, for some reason, they waited till midnight;
Well, a few minutes before if I'm being really honest;
Celebration was about to break into night.

Soon they all went mad and poured themselves whisky,
Which is also Scottish or Scotch, I have learned.
They sang something foreign, called, I think, Auld Lang
Syne;
Then Grandma said she thought some rest I had earned.

She suggested that I might like to take to my bed
And the rest of the family would follow quite soon.
I heard them still partying as I went off to sleep;
I suspected I'd not see them again until noon.

But I'd had a good time even though it was strange

And quite different from what I'd experienced before.

But I'd buy a CD of that weird Scottish music

If next year I could stay up to find out a bit more.

Temptation

In the playground at school, someone offered me tablets;
They said those I really should try;
That they'd take away all my grief, cares and worries
And lift me to a completely new high.

I admit I was tempted because I was feeling quite down
And would have welcomed some easy solution.
The man said that I would never see a downside
And would experience no retribution.

He wanted some money, just to cover his costs,
Because he was basically quite kind.
He said he hated those who exploited the young
But would help them new pleasures to find.

I was not really sure and had no money to hand
So decided to wait for a while.
But my best friend was keen and gave all her money;
She took the tablets; he left with a smile.

For no very good reason, I did not see him again
And continued my life as before.
Soon after, my friend began to be absent from school,
With behaviour no-one could ignore.

She was seen on street corners looking desperate and ill,
Doing anything that would get her some money.
Some said that they'd seen the man with her again
But, when cars came, he left in a hurry.

I was approached many times over the next several years
By people offering some instant heaven.
But always I remembered my best friend from school;
She'd provided the very best lesson.

At Home and Away

When I heard my child singing in the choir,
At the Christmas concert in the school,
I was shocked; she seemed inspired and on fire,
Quite different from the tomboy at home.

When I saw her play in the volleyball team,
She ran round like a person possessed.
I could not rid my mind of the thought that it seemed
Until now I'd not seen her true worth.

When I saw my son play key part in a play,
His speeches were full of expression.
How different that seemed from our dull, normal day,
When we'd eat dinner and watch television.

He took a camera when he went on school trip
And back home he showed us the photos.
The quality of his pictures quite easily outstripped
Anything we took on our family holidays.

My daughter and boyfriend, my son with his girl:
So vibrant, so joyous, so normal.
It seemed that they lived their life in a whirl;
Back home, they seemed always so quiet.

Their lives, their loves, their adventures, their fun
Looked always more joy far from home.
But I have to say, when all's said and done,
That their love always came back to us.

When I Was Young

When I was young I thought me quite big;
Then when I was older, I felt horribly small.
But I grew and I grew, in mind and in body
And suddenly found I was really quite tall.

As a child, I played on merry-go-rounds,
Had stuffed animals as friends and mechanical toys.
For a while, I grew up and rejected the nonsense,
Then reunited with things that still gave me joy.

Each year, I had parties in wild fancy dress
But I grew to appreciate clothes more refined.
I was seriously cool, my demeanour controlled,
Until I wanted again my childhood to find.

As I grew up, I found things quite challenging;
It seemed people expected so much from me.
I felt like a child in the guise of an adult,
Instead of an adult who from childhood broke free.

But now more mature, I have worked out the answer:

Learn and act from the years that you've had;

Think and behave like the adult you are

But cherish inner childhood, reflect and be glad.